Pieces of My Heart

~♡~

Poems of Love, Loss, and Longing

Gail Harris

Pinion Press
Blue Springs, Mississippi

Gail Harris

Library of Congress Control Number: 2007938273

Harris, Gail
Pieces of My Heart: Poems of Love,
Loss, and Longing/Gail Harris
First Edition

ISBN 978-0-9770201-2-6

Published by Pinion Press
1754 CR 278, Suite 102 Blue Springs, MS 38828

Printed in the United States

Cover design by Jonathan Gullery
Cover photography by Darrell Ivy
Graphic design by Zachary Moore

I dedicate this book

to my mother,

Sara,

and to the memory

of my father,

Bud Harris

Mom, you will always have

a very big piece of my heart.

I love you, always...

Gail

Acknowledgements

This book of poetry is something my mom has encouraged me to do for years, and I thank her from the bottom of my heart for her unconditional love and support, and most of all, for her constant praise and encouragement through the years. Her love shines through her beauty and her soul. Without her, I would have never been able to accomplish this.

A very special thanks goes to my friend, Leanna Lindsey Hollis, M.D., who believed in me, and without hesitation offered to help publish these. Also, many thanks to Leanna's son, Ryan, for his technical support on the computer. I want to thank Sue Simpson, whose death is the reason Leanna and I reconnected. Only Sue would see the humor in that!

I want to thank my brothers, Bob and Glen, my best friends in the world. I thank them for the fathers they've become, so much like our own father.

I thank my Dad, who was always there for me, who is looking down from heaven, I'm sure, cheering me on. I was a 'Daddy's girl', in all my fragile moments, and his life, his fun-loving sense of humor, and integrity taught me more than I can convey in words.

I thank my soul mate, the true love of my life, Steve Brandon, for his constant love, and all the magical moments we share, some of which I have shared with you. I look forward to living in our cottage by the sea some day.

I tried to put these pieces of my heart back together. Here are some of them for you...

Table Of Contents

Love

Loss

Longing

Love

My Mother's Love

I've never known a love so sweet,
So pure, so understanding
I smile each time I touch her cheek,
And feel her love unending.
She's taught me what I know of love
Through her unselfish caring.
I dare not think where I might be
Without her hand to guide me.
Not once has she put her own needs
Above those of her family.
Few words describe her acts of love,
Her beauty, beyond measure.
I've hidden in my heart a thousand
Moments I can treasure.
It's hard to grasp this love she gives,
It's beyond all thoughts or words.
I watched my father glow with love
Each time his eyes met hers.
He was a happy man each day
He had with her on earth,
And now my brothers' children's faces
Beam with love for her.
Their legacy of love continues now year after year.
I have my mother's smile they say,
I hope to have her heart someday...
Her kind and gentle, loving way,
And all that makes her mine.
She is my lifeline, confidant, and
Best friend in the world.
And even now, I still can be
Her 'only little girl'.

My Greatest Teacher

Faith and Courage
Walked hand in hand
In the life and soul of this wise man.
Whatever seemed to come his way
He took in stride day to day.
I asked him if he questioned 'Why?'
And with his faith came his reply,
"I have never questioned 'Why?'
For God knows so much more than I
He says it rains on all of us,
Those who are just, and those unjust."
He was my greatest teacher,
Not of books or worldly things,
He taught me about trees and birds,
He taught me how to sing...
He taught me about laughter,
And the warmth a marriage brings.
He taught me about hope,
And family ties, and things.
He taught me through the life he lived,
Consistent and so pure,
He taught me how to not give up,
He taught me to endure.
Faith and Courage
Walked hand in hand
In the life and soul of this wise man.
He was my greatest teacher
Above any scholar, writer, preacher.
A hero in this life of mine,
My father and friend for all time.

11

A Dandelion's Dance

I closed my eyes
I made a wish,
A special wish for you.
I watched each part,
And saw my heart
Float in the wind
With yours...
Dancing around
Above the ground
So soft, so free, and pure.
A perfect dandelion's dance
With just one breath
Becomes romance.
A wish, a hope,
A dream-come-true,
A perfect wish
I wished for you.
I saw your heart
In just one glance.
May I have this dance,
My love?
A dandelion's dance...
This perfect wish
I wished for you,
You are a dream-come-true.

This Butterfly

~ ♡ ~

The sun is glistening on my skin
With tiny drops of oil and water.
I lie here reading as you fly to greet me,
A familiar meeting,
A simple greeting.
This spring I find myself content
As this butterfly comes to greet me.
I don't long so much to fly away
Perhaps forever, perhaps to stay...
Instead I'm touched,
Because it seems to want to stay with me
As long as it can sit there
Until the wind just takes its wings.
I feel a strange connection
With no words, but deep affection.
I cannot fly, it cannot help but fly...
Yet for a moment
We are one.
No longer do I live to dream
Of only flying,
And this spring I find myself content
As I have never been.
Perhaps I've found a way to fly,
To soar among the clouds, the sky,
To live among the butterflies
Through your heart, my love,
And somehow through your eyes.
You take me there, I'm unaware of time,
Or where we'll go.
I close my eyes and realize
That finally I can fly.

Soul Mates

~ ♡ ~

After all these years
I'm standing here
To pledge my love to you, my dear.
Though youth has stolen
Half our lives
I'll watch the sunset in your eyes.
Life won't be built on yesterdays,
But from right now, starting today,
I have no fear of what may come
For God is joining us as one.
I take your hand
To walk upon this road of love
As we are one.
Our memories and family bonds
We'll cherish all our days beyond,
And as we pledge these vows today
I promise I will always stay.
I'll never leave you or forsake
These holy vows that we will make.
So many years I've waited for
This second chance,
Our sweet romance.
I realize it must be fate,
I've finally found my one soul mate.
As we grow old together, Love,
I pray for wisdom from above,
That God will keep us just this close...
And He will teach us
How to love.

for Steve

On Valentine's

If you call my name out loud
I will hear you, Love,
And if you whisper in the wind
It will drift my way.
If you dream of me, my love,
Softly as you sleep,
I will meet you in your dreams,
We will be complete.
If you're standing in the cold,
You are not alone.
I will keep you warm, and wrap
My loving arms around you.
If you need some time alone,
I'll be here when you get home.
Gather all your thoughts together,
There's no storm
That we can't weather.
If you need a friend, my love,
I will help you to discover
All that we can be together.
You and me,
Always, forever.
All through our lives I'll take the time
To thank God
For this love of mine.
Not just on Valentine's
This year,
But every day
That we spend here.

Today

When I look into your eyes
I see a thousand smiles.
You adore me
Like no other one has
My whole life.
You take away my worries
And I can throw away my cares
Because you're there,
And I'm right here.
And if I never saw your face again,
I've memorized your eyes.
And if I never felt your touch again,
I'd love you all my life.
And if I had to choose
One day with you,
I would sacrifice tomorrow
Just to have
Today,
Just to feel this way
Today.
If I tried to figure out
The reason you're still here,
I might waste a moment
Of the love
You and I share,
So I'll just live
Today
While you are here
Right by my side
Because I know I'll never find
Another you in my life.

Beyond Eternity

Yesterday just doesn't mean
That much to me.
All those crazy, mixed up dreams
Just weren't meant to be.
In all my plans
You are the only man I want to see,
So if you want to walk this road with me,
Then take my hand.
We'll go as far as love will take us,
As far as we can see,
And then we'll close our eyes,
And go beyond eternity.
We'll soar among the clouds,
Only come down if we can't breathe,
We'll float among a million stars,
Smile at the moon, just you and me.
Our love will live beyond eternity.
Nothing before the two of us
Has any kind of meaning,
And from this day forward, I promise,
You will have
My heart.
May nothing come
Before our love
As we begin our lives together.
Let's begin again,
Today, my love.

for Steve

One More Day

If I had only one more day,
If there were no more words to say,
And if our paths never crossed again
I'd have no regrets, and I could never forget
All the things that we have said and done.
I've held you closer than anyone.
I've touched you and
Your passion for life itself.
And if I had only one more day with you,
I know we'd find out
Something new about each other,
And we would have another
Sweet memory to share.
I would be right there with you,
Forever in your heart.
You would have a part of me
To keep with you for eternity.
And if I had only one more day with you,
You know I'd have to cry.
I can't imagine
Having to say goodbye...
But if I had only
One more day with you,
I'd want to try to give you
All the love I have inside.
I've saved it my entire life
For you, my love,
You're all I've ever dreamed of.
Only promise me
More than just one more day.

Inside My Heart

Inside my heart
There is a part
That's only yours.
It's always there
Whether you are near
Or far away.
I'd hoped someday
That I would know
This kind of love,
And here you are
Inside my heart.
Your gentle love
Takes me away
From where I am
To higher ground
Where I can soar
Because I've found
A love with wings,
Teaching me things
I thought I'd never learn,
And through your words
I've heard the many things
You've said to me.
You've touched a place
Inside my heart
I thought I'd never feel,
And through your words
You've played this melody
Inside of me.
Inside my heart
Is where you are.

Ode to My Parents

You let us go
One by one
Your baby boy,
Your only daughter,
And your first-born son.
Your love made us
What we've become
A part of you,
And yet we're one,
Individuals, now on our own.
Your hugs, caresses, the way
You've blessed us
The ups, the downs,
The all night stresses.
Life's blows cannot compare or measure,
Our love's endured
Through family treasures.
We've dreamed big dreams,
We've won, we've lost.
We've laughed and loved,
And paid the cost.
Someday through children
Of our own, we'll know
That kind of love you've known.
Until then, the sacrifice is your own.
Thank you, dear parents,
For love, for
Home.

for Mom and Dad

After 40 Years

⁓ ♡ ⁓

They built their home on this old place.
He worked the land with his two hands
And she was always there,
Right by his side.
Believing in the things he said
She was everything he needed,
And he always treated her
Just like a queen.
They have the kind of love
That lasts forever
The kind that none of us know whether
We will ever find in this lifetime.
And after forty years
They still hold hands,
They're still lovers and best friends.
They have the kind of love that never ends,
Even after forty years.
Just a few years down the road
Their family started to grow,
They were blessed with two boys and a girl.
Even though their world was changing
The love between them only grew stronger,
It was no longer just the two of them.
Time is passing quickly
And the years are rolling by,
But she still sees that love in his eyes,
Even after forty years...

for Mom and Dad

My Big Brother

Dear Lord,
Please take good care of him,
My strong, courageous friend.
He's been here for me
My whole life,
And will be 'til the end.
No words can soothe
This hurt he feels,
Or take away his pain.
He lives so far away, you see,
A phone call's not the same.
I pray these prayers
For him each day
When I don't know
Just what to say.
I've been there, Lord,
I know how hard
This is for him,
Day after day.
And yet, he has this little soul
To guide along her way,
An innocent and precious child
Who sometimes feels afraid.
Protect her, Lord,
And keep her safe.
Protect her from this pain,
That she might feel
So loved inside,
So no innocence is lost.

Too many things
Have happened now,
To try to bridge the gap,
Too many lies, too much deceit,
What's left is fear and doubt.
Replace each question
With your answers,
Each doubt with certainty,
And take away his fear, Dear Lord,
And give him sweet release.
I place my brother in Your hands,
This strong, yet gentle man.
I thank You for the wisdom
You have laid upon his plans.
I thank You for the father
He's become to this sweet one.
He reminds me so of Daddy,
The greatest father
We could have known.
Please bless him, God,
And guide him through this
To the end.
He's not only
My big brother,
He's my very special friend.

for Glen

A Sister and Her Brother

~ ♡ ~

There are bonds
We struggle with on earth
To try to keep alive,
Then there are those
We search for
To help us to survive.
Some bonds
Are gifts from birth,
And effortlessly strive
Within no boundaries or walls
Yet affect us all our lives.
I once read
Where our families
Don't grow up necessarily
Under just one roof.
That might be true
I have no proof,
For I am one
Whom God decided
This gift should be from birth...
A lasting bond,
A younger brother's love
To share on earth.
He had such a sweetness
From the day
That he was born.
I made sure, instantly,
He'd always be informed
That I was right,
He had an awful lot to learn.

It seems like
All those years
Passed by so quickly
Now, today.
He grew up, had a family,
And moved away.
As I look back I realize
How much
That he taught me,
But he was always
Far beyond his years
Our mom would say.
He has a special gift
Of healing lives,
A surgeon's hands.
So many people count on him,
He is a strong, wise man.
Our past
Is intertwined with love
And memories combined.
A better bond between
A sister and her brother
Is hard to find.

for Bob

Our Precious Baby

~ ♡ ~

Will he have your eyes, Love?
Will she have my smile?
The moment that we hold him
Will just be for a while.
She'll become a beauty
And marry someone someday,
But no matter what, or how old they are,
They'll always be our precious baby.
This life inside of me
Will soon become reality,
A precious baby born of love
Between my love and me.
The dream that I've been dreaming
All my life for many years,
Will soon become a part of us
Through laughter and some tears.
When we first fell in love,
And knew our souls had met,
The conversations that we had
I never will forget, the way you looked at me
When we talked about a family.
I imagined Sunday afternoons,
And picnics in the park.
I pictured our children
As I held you in the dark,
And soon the day will come
When we will hold our daughter, or our son.
Every morning I count the days
Until our baby will be born.

for Myriam

Connor's Christening Prayer

The love you've brought our families,
The wonder that you are,
The life you have ahead of you,
Your eyes that shine like stars.
A legacy of love surrounds you
To help you on your way,
Toward life and opportunities far beyond today.
Some of us are blessed to hold you
In our arms today,
While some of us must hold you
From much farther away...
There are eyes in Heaven
Watching over you today,
And there are prayers from
Loved ones who are far away.
Still the love that God has blessed
You with will someday make you strong,
As you grow into a man,
And discover that you belong
To this legacy of love
Between your parents and their son,
From generations long ago
And all those yet to come.
So on this day of promises
To guide you as you grow,
The love that we all have for you
Is more than you can know.
God bless you, our dear Connor,
And keep you safe from above,
As we celebrate today from our
Legacy of Love.

for Connor

I'm Whispering This Prayer

Simple wishes
Hershey kisses
Stardust in your eyes
Mommie's laughter
Ever-after
Daddy's little girl...
London bridges
Sunlit beaches
Glistening in your eyes
Harvest moons
Picnics in June
Awaiting some surprise.
I'm whispering this prayer for you,
Of love and hope
In all you do.
For dreams and fairy tales
Come true,
For happiness and laughter, too.
I'm whispering this prayer for you,
For the woman
You will grow into,
For strength from God,
A humble heart,
For wisdom,
And much gratitude.
For guidance, and some solitude,
I'm whispering this prayer for you.
Ponytails
And satin ribbons
Sunday dresses
Sweet caresses
White lace, and Mom's perfume

High-heeled shoes
And dressing up
On lazy afternoons.
Homemade cookies
Shopping sprees
First love, and
Skinned-up knees.
Porcelain dolls
And Mommie's make-up
Broken hearts and
Trying to break up.
Puffy clouds
With smiling faces
Learning all the social graces
Lemonade and summertime
Memories to make
In time...
I'm whispering this prayer for you,
Of love and hope
In all you do.

for Madelyn

A Lullaby

If I could give you eyes
To see yourself
The way I do,
If I could say something
To you to make you smile again,
If I could hold your hand,
And tell you everything
Will be all right,
If I could kiss you
On the cheek,
Sing you a lullaby...
But since you're far away,
Then I'll just say a prayer for you,
That God will keep you safe,
And wrap His loving arms around you.
And when I softly say this prayer,
Even though I'm not there,
I know God will keep you
In His care.
If I could wipe away your tears
That you have cried tonight,
If I could listen to your hurts,
If I could see your eyes,
If I could hold you
When you're scared,
Then it would ease my mind.
If I could kiss you
On the cheek,
Sing you a lullaby...

for Marlee

Wishes

~ ♡ ~

I wish you laughter
To fill your days
When smiles are hard to find.
I wish you music
To sing in your heart
When the world seems so unkind.
I wish you melodies of love
From people you will meet
To help you deal with sadness
If you face defeat.
I wish you lyrics that come out of
Conversations of your past
To remind you of the good things,
Not those that didn't last.
I wish you friendship, one that's true,
Whenever you need someone to talk to.
I wish you time alone sometimes
To hear the music in your mind
When things are going much too fast,
And you have to have
Some peace and rest.
I wish you eyes to see your gifts
So you can give away
All the love that is within you,
It wasn't meant to stay.
And most of all
I wish the music of your life
Will always be
A dream that keeps you going,
And a love that sets you free.

for Marlee

My Little Blue and Blackie

~ ♡ ~

I met her on one sunny day in March as I recall,
Her eyes were round and big as saucers,
And yellow as the sun.
Her hair as black as night,
And as smooth as finest silk
She always looked surprised,
And ran everywhere she went.
And then I met her sister,
And she, too, stole my heart.
Her eyes were bluer than any sky I'd ever seen.
Those blue eyes mesmerized me,
And matched her long, blue fur.
She had a certain sweetness in her tiny little face,
As if to say she needed me,
But it was I who needed her...
They both loved me instantly,
And trusted me for everything.
These two baby sisters, once little balls of fur,
Born opposite in nature, but identical in purr.
One black, and wild, and daring,
One blue, and calm, and caring.
Sometimes reverse their personalities,
A mystery all their own...
These little furry angels take such good care of me.
They're always glad when I get home,
And never ask for much,
Just treats and food and water,
And lots and lots of love.
They love me unconditionally,
As I love both of them.
My little Blue and Blackie,
To think, I got you on a whim!

My Sweet Cousin Irene

To know her is to love her,
A friend to everyone.
She never meets a stranger,
And her haven is her home.
Like the flowers in her garden,
So delicate and new,
Their freshness and their beauty
Will live on in those she knew.
She showers us with beauty
As her hands meet Mother Earth,
And reminds us of the lilies
And how much each one is worth.
Her elegance shines each time
Her roses are in bloom,
And with each bouquet she gives away
You know she'll be back soon!
Her bright blue eyes begin to dance
As talk of spring is near.
A thousand daffodils come home
To live with 'Mother Dear'.
As the iris blooms so gracefully
So does this special friend,
Each time she fills your heart with love
And a fragrance that won't end.
And like the flowers in her garden,
Always swaying with the wind,
They soothe our souls as we behold
The freedom that they bring.
And when I see a flower, so soft and so serene,
I'll smile and always think of you,
My sweet Cousin Irene.

The Strongest Man I've Ever Known

The strongest man I've ever known,
Who sings to me the sweetest songs,
The one I've loved my whole life long,
Who taught me right from wrong,
His blue eyes sparkle when he laughs,
They shine like stars against the path
Of those he meets along the way.
He's so much fun, you wish he'd stay.
His one true love adores him so,
And if you saw them you would know,
For tenderness so pure just shows,
And a love like theirs continually grows.
From two sons and a daughter,
A grandson and two granddaughters followed.
They light our lives with so much joy
Two baby girls, and a little boy.
No regrets come to mind,
Only one wish...that I could stop time.
For we have loved, and we have lived
With so much more than wealth could give.
You gave us more than fame and fortune,
We have your heart, and your devotion,
Your secret to life, your magic potion.
Through the years we've seen firsthand
An undying love between a woman and a man.
A gift so rare, few understand,
But from the beginning this was your plan.
You are the strongest man I've ever known,
You've given me the sweetest songs,
And I've loved you my whole life long.
Dad, I'll never let you go.

You Stayed

~ ♡ ~

My best friend, confidant, and
Counselor for sure
Believe me, you're a thousand things
And more.
My heart is tied to yours,
You almost know my thoughts.
You've taught me about things
That can't be bought.
And when I've lost my way,
It's been you who stayed
To help get back the 'me'
I used to be.
Don't think I haven't noticed
All the sacrifices made
By you alone,
And all the times you've prayed.
Thank God you stayed.
A gracefulness and beauty
Shines so bright
Inside your eyes,
Your gentleness and faith
Are such a part
Of your sweet life.
No matter where I've been,
Or where I'll go
On down the road,
You'll be right there beside me
Always cheering me on.
Thank God you stayed.

for Mom

A Prayer for Terry

To some he's just a doctor, to me he is a man.
I call him by his first name,
Because he is my friend.
I've watched him grow in mind and soul
For several years now, Lord.
He's been there for my family
Through many winters dark and cold.
At first I only saw his eyes, so blue and full of life,
I saw how being perfect
On the outside caused him strife.
And then I saw the beauty of the artist in his soul.
His hands created art from all kinds
Of wood for young and old.
I watch him now as he performs his magic on this race
Of human lives who look to him
For knowledge and Your grace.
Dear Lord, my father loved him
As if he were his own,
And while we had him here on earth,
He treated him like a son.
And now he's touched my mother's life
With healing hands of love.
Dear God, I pray you'll give him
Perfect wisdom from above.
The trials that we have on earth
Grow harder now with age.
He's had his own, please keep him strong,
And give him peace today.
I thank You, God, for this young man
You've placed in all our lives.
I count him as my family, as I will all my life.

for Terry Pinson, M.D.

So Close

I want to hear Your voice,
I want to know Your way,
I want to do what's right, dear Lord,
Give me the words to say.
Keep me so close to You, dear Lord,
So easy just to fall.
Help me to keep my eyes on You,
Oh God, I hear Your call.
I know I'm nothing without You,
There's nothing good in me.
I trust You Lord, with all my heart,
Direct my path today.
Help me to keep my mind on You,
Think only on those things
That give Your peace, Your honesty,
Your love that strengthens me.
Keep me so close to You, dear Lord,
And catch me lest I fall
So far that I can't get back up,
Back to where You are.
Keep me on that straight and narrow path
That I must trod.
Give me light to walk upon
That road with You, my God.
Please keep me so close
That You will never
Let me go.
Away from You
Is somewhere that
I never want to know.

Best Friends

Reflecting on friendships
Now and those past,
Some have grown stronger, some didn't last.
Friendship can be fragile, and it can be tough,
We go through some good times
While others can get rough.
Your friendship is truly a gift to me.
Through your eyes, I've come to really see
How trust can become a way of life,
No matter how much time or strife
It takes to give again.
Through a change of plans
Comes a second chance,
A brand new start, a change of heart.
We've laughed and cried, and tried to hide
Some things we couldn't face.
We've learned how time takes care of things
And even can erase the scars,
The pain, the fear of love.
We've learned to trust in God above,
Even though there are still times
When we're unsure of the plans He has for us.
If there were words I'd write them down,
To thank God for my friend I've found.
Sometimes we speak without a sound,
Sometimes there's laughter all around.
We've had some great times, and some bad,
But of all our fun times, and even the sad,
I've discovered this beautiful friend,
I'm so glad, for you are
The sister that I never had.

for Linda

Smiles, and Warmth and Dreams

For smiles, and warmth and dreams,
It's those, you see, that mean the most to me,
And you, my friend, have given time and time again
More than your share.
I know you're always there
With smiles, and warmth and dreams.
There's only now, we've figured out,
Through all our conversations.
We've talked of love, and life and more,
And looked into the future.
Our past has taught us much,
And yet we've so much more to learn.
To live today is all there is,
We've had our share of fun.
For smiles, and warmth and dreams,
It's those, you see, that mean the most to me,
And you, my friend, have given time and time again
More than your share.
I know you're always there
With smiles, and warmth and dreams.
When people demand too much of me,
You're always there with what I need,
A lighter look on everything,
And where to take what burdens me.
Your faith, your trust, your gentle touch,
Your giving, without taking
Have earned a special place in me,
And when my heart is breaking,
I come to you
For smiles, and warmth,
And dreams.

Our Mittie

~ ♡ ~

Five feet tall, she's seen it all, almost a century.
So spry, so cute, so interesting,
Intelligence befalls
The stories that she has to share,
The places that she's seen and been,
I want to keep on listening,
So I can learn the secret to her
Long and happy life on earth.
Her recipes, her family, her upbeat attitude,
Her church, her faith, her independence,
And her love.
Her sense of humor,
And the way she's always on the go,
She never stops, unless of course,
Someone's in need she knows.
Exercise and gardening,
Baking cookies, always reading,
Still driving, yes, running around,
It's hard to keep up with our Mittie.
She's like a cat, you know,
I told her once she has nine lives.
She just looked at me, and laughed,
Turned her head and smiled.
I've loved the laughs we've had together,
She's someone I adore.
Would you believe our Mittie
Is now ninety-four?
She's sharper than most anyone
That I have ever known.
Someday I hope that I deserve
To be so well-preserved!

for Mittie

I Meant To...

~ ♡ ~

I meant to say I loved you
On Valentine's this year.
I meant to send an Easter card
Because you are so dear.
I thought about your birthday,
And forgot to call you then...
I knew that you'd forgive me
Because we're such good friends.
After I finished that last hot dog,
I thought you'd have had fun.
That 4th of July just passed right by
A holiday, another one...
Labor Day I meant to have you over,
If just for coffee,
But I got side-tracked, and wouldn't you know
There was somewhere else I had to go...
This Thanksgiving
I had the sweetest thoughts of you...
I meant to write them down,
But something came up, I don't remember,
Think I went out of town...
So now that Christmas
Has rolled around
I've finished shopping, and here I am!
I've tried all year to let you know
How special you are...
I love you so...
Well, once again
Life's been so hard...
So here's your
Belated Christmas card!

O Wise One

~ ♡ ~

O, Wise One,
Whose advise is never taken,
Please speak to me,
So blatant and assured.
I want to listen to you, now...
Just can't seem to slow down somehow.
0, Wise One,
Whose advise is never taken,
Why do you waste your time on me?
A peon, an earthly one
Who can't seem to be free
Of worries, cares, and anger.
Why me?
0, Wise One,
Whose advise is never taken,
I pray to learn to listen,
And not to speak so quickly,
Free me of this emotion.
My devotion is somewhat twisted,
And devoured greatly.
0, Wise One,
Whose advice is never taken,
Teach me, lest I'm shaken
To the cavity of my heart.
A part of me has ears that
Want to hear,
And fear what I might learn.
0, Wise One,
Whose advise is never taken,
Am I mistaken,
Or did You say
You loved me?

Your Strength

Your strength goes far beyond
The weaknesses in me.
I know You are the Way,
Your Truth
Can set me free.
You gave Your everything,
And died just for me.
The least that I can do
Is live my life for You.
Take the things
That weigh me down,
Take my life
Turn it around.
Make me more like You,
Dear Lord, I know
That I cannot afford
To live my life without
The strength that comes
From knowing You.
Dear God, I truly want
To know You.
There are things
That hold me back,
Things I know I lack,
But You have overcome it all,
You are the higher call.
You gave Your everything,
And died just for me.
The least that I can do
Is live my life for You.

An Old Friend

If you're feeling
Just a little bit downhearted,
And you can't remember
How or when it started,
And you find yourself
Wishing for an old friend,
Just pick up the phone
And call me right then.
There's no other love
Sweeter than an old friend,
And it's the one love
You can count on
That will never end.
Whenever you need
A shoulder to cry on,
You can be sure
There's no love sweeter
Than an old friend.
It always makes me smile
To think about the good times,
And the promises we made
That things would always be just fine.
The way you made me laugh
Like no one else could,
And that twinkle in your eye
When you were up to no good!
There's no other love
Sweeter than an old friend,
And it's the one love you can count on
That will never end,
My old friend, my old friend.

for Rhonda

Kindred Spirits

Such gentleness,
A precious gift from you to me.
You gave so freely,
Unselfishly, and helped me to finally see
It really doesn't matter
So much what our plot in life may be.
What matters most is
Who and what, and how much
We choose to see.
For many years I searched and searched
For answers painfully.
I questioned 'Why?'
And bitterness engulfed
My soul and me.
Yet today our kindred spirits met,
And you became my song
Of life and love and laughter,
And a kind and gentle strong.
Your gift, so rare,
I thank you for,
Please never, ever change.
And when you feel
That life's too much,
Or just a bit too strange,
Remember me,
That day we met,
And somehow picture me,
And feel my spirit
As I fly.
You helped to set me free!

for Melissa

Is She Your Soul Mate?

Do you long to hear her voice
When the day is almost gone?
Do you rush to finish work
So that you can hurry home?
Do you whisper little secrets
Only the two of you can share?
Do you laugh a lot together,
Would you take her anywhere?
Does she take your breath away
When she walks into the room?
Can you picture
Walking down the aisle,
She's your bride,
And you're her groom?
When you look around your house,
Is there any extra room?
Does she sweep you
Off your feet,
And take you straight up
To the moon?
Do her lips capture your spirit
When you kiss them tenderly?
Do you feel a tiny thrill
When she touches you
On the sleeve?
Does she give you your freedom,
Or do you sometimes want to leave?
Is there a longing for her
In your soul?
Does she complete you,
Make you whole?

When you look into the future,
Way on down the road,
Is she there with you
When you're old?
When beauty fades,
Time's been unkind,
Is she the one
You want to find?
To share your life,
To be your wife,
You know, forever
Is a long, long, time.
Please be sure,
Dear friend of mine,
Remember,
Love has no deadlines.
Makes no demands
Of its own way,
Is never rude,
But patient and kind.
A soul mate is what
I hope you find,
But sometimes it's wise
To take your time.

Let Them See Your Love

Let them see Your love inside of me,
Teach me what I can and cannot be.
Show me in Your Word so I can see,
How You really live inside of me.
Let them see Your love in spite of me.
Let them see the part of You that cares,
When their hearts are pained with doubts and fears.
Let me be Your hands so You can serve,
Every need they have, I'm Yours to serve.
Let them see Your love in spite of me.
Let me hear, and listen to their hurts,
Know when to speak, and when to use Your words.
Take what is said, what only You can hear
Help me listen, let me be Your ears
Let them see Your love in spite of me.
Let them see Your heart, and how it bleeds,
To show them You can meet their every need.
Take my eyes, and open them to see,
That when we know the truth, it sets us free.
Let them see Your love in spite of me.
Let them see the Truth inside of me,
You are all I am, and hope to be.
Let them see there's nothing good in me.
Make me more like You, so they can see
Your love, in spite of me.
Take my arms and use them to embrace
The lonely, scarred, rejected, and disgraced.
Take my voice, and use it Lord, to praise
Your holy name, to sing of all Your grace.
Let them see Your love
In spite of me.

for my students

That Magic

Remember springtime,
The air was sweet
In the afternoons...
Remember Sundays,
The conversations we had in June.
Remember autumn,
And the leaves falling all around.
And in December,
We bowed our heads
On that Christmas Eve,
And now it's all coming back around again...
Here are the moments
That I saved for you,
Here are the memories
That they have brought us to,
And here's the magic
That made me fall in love with you,
And best of all,
The rest of my life
I give to you.
When we're much older,
I know you'll still
Take my breath away,
And every springtime,
I know our love will never fade,
And when it's December,
And life may seem a little cold,
You'll slip your hand in mine,
And I'll still hold you tightly,
Because we have that magic.

Your Poetry in Motion

I feel this ocean inside of me,
Flowing with peace and honesty
Where rainbows live,
And sunsets too,
The way I feel
When I'm with you.
I close my eyes,
And feel the waves,
Believe in dreams and better days,
And somehow
In this dream-like state,
I always seem to see your face.
There's magic in your touch,
It's filled with such emotion,
And there's music in your eyes,
As they dance
Each time you smile.
Your poetry in motion,
Each line I try to read,
It's hard to grasp it all at once,
I'll take just what I need.
Pieces of our conversations
Keep coming back to me
Like whispers in the wind,
They echo tenderly.
I hear your voice
When you're not here.
I feel your touch,
And have no fear.

So many times
I pray this prayer,
That God will keep you
In His care,
And He will somehow
Keep you here
So close and near to me.
I pray we won't change
With the seasons,
In winter, spring or fall,
That you will stay
Close to my heart,
And never change at all.
Your poetry in motion
Is something that I need.
I wish for summer always
With few dark and hazy days.
If promises aren't broken,
And wishes can come true,
The most that I can hope for
Is that I will always know you.

Our Cottage by the Sea

Feel the sun upon your face,
Watch it glisten on the sand.
See the waves upon the sea,
Taste the salt
When you kissed me.
Catch a glimpse
Of that first sunset,
Hear the ocean speak to you,
And in that very moment
Remember that I love you, too.
And when the sun
Begins to fade,
And you hear the music play,
And we both begin to age,
Let's go there, Love, to stay.
Have our cottage by the sea,
Just my love right there with me.
Having coffee in the morning,
Holding hands and feeling free.
Quiet nights and peaceful days,
Time to laugh and time to play,
No real worries anymore,
So content there by the shore.
Building castles in the sand,
I reach out,
You take my hand.
Just us two,
My love and me,
In our cottage by the sea.

for Steve

The Music Box

~ ♡ ~

It was a cold November day,
November 28th.
A day I dreaded most for her,
The first anniversary she'd spent
Without him...
If you've ever lost someone you love
You know the 'first' is always the worst.
First birthday, Christmas, Father's Day,
And anniversary.
My father died six months before,
Thanksgiving had come and gone.
I spent the night
At home with Mom
So she wouldn't be alone.
The holidays that year were hard
To say the least.
We'd tried to shop for Christmas gifts
To take our mind off things.
You'd have to know my parents,
And the kind of love they shared,
To know the loss she suffered
When one day, he wasn't there.
They had a kind of magic
Between the two of them,
Something all their own,
That lasted through the years.
Even his last week on earth,
I saw that twinkle in his eyes
When she leaned down to kiss him
Each time they said goodbye.

I loved to watch them laugh
About some ordinary thing.
I loved the way that they held hands,
The looks that passed between them.
I knew that she'd remember
All these things
That cold November.
How could I comfort my own mom,
When I, too, was still grieving?
We woke up very early,
And put the coffee on.
No T.V., just the silence
Of the day surrounded us.
Then suddenly we heard
The music box he'd given her.
The notes rang clear,
And we could hear
Their favorite song was playing.
In all the years before 'til then,
It never just came on,
Yet in the stillness
Of that morning
It played alone,
Completely through their song.
She looked at me,
I looked at her,
As music filtered
Through the silence,
And we both stood still
In disbelief
As we turned toward
The music box
My Dad had given her.

It continued playing,
Yet no one had wound it up,
Or turned it on.
Oh! What a gift!
We hugged, we cried, and realized
Had we been one, not two,
No one would have believed us,
That on November 28th,
That very special day,
My Dad had 'arranged'
To have that music box play.
Of course, it was his own unique
And mystical way...
His spirit filled us, and the room,
A mystery consumed us both.
I'm sure that was his plan.
I know my Mom would tell you,
He was a very special man.
The music came and went that day,
The memory still plays
Inside our hearts
On many days,
But especially
On November 28th.

for Mom

Loss

Old Perfume

Rolled into the driveway,
Parked the car in that same spot.
Walked up to the house,
Turned the key, and went on in.
The house was much too quiet,
No familiar voices there,
I headed for the closet
To decide what I should wear.
Saw the poet's blouse you gave me,
It smelled like old perfume.
The sheer and soft cream-colored one,
Remembered when we danced 'til dawn.
We finally made it home,
And almost spent the night outside.
You were laughing at the moon
On that summer night in June.
It smelled like old perfume,
And when it filled the room
It took me back in time
To days gone by.
It smelled like old perfume,
And when I thought about that night I had to cry,
All because I smelled that old perfume.
It's hard to put my make-up on,
The tears they just won't stop,
Knowing he'll be here at nine o'clock.
I don't know what to wear,
And I don't care, I shouldn't go.
There's one blouse that I know
I won't be wearing though,
It smelled like old perfume...

No Time

Once I thought we had forever,
And time was on our side.
I remember how you loved me,
I could see it in your eyes.
Something changed,
And you became
Someone I never even knew.
How could Father Time have been
So cruel to me and you?
Now there's no time
To say 'I'm sorry',
There's no time to understand.
There's no time to take it back,
No time to make another plan.
There's no time to say 'If only',
And no time for sad regrets.
There's no time
For you and me now,
Only time to just forget.
How did time
Slip through our fingers?
When did we begin to fade
Into a world beyond the one
That you and I had made?
And what makes this one better?
It's no easier today.
On down the road
I'm sure that we
Will make the same mistakes,
But there's no time.

Forgotten Dreams

Saw an old friend
That we used to know today,
And when I turned to go,
I could have sworn I saw your face.
And as I ran across the street
I realized it wasn't you,
And we would probably
Never meet again.
Forgotten dreams, reminding me
Of all the plans that we once made
When you were free, and I was
All you wanted me to be.
Forgotten dreams...
Went back to a place we used to go today.
Thought about the night it snowed,
You held me like you'd never let me go.
After that night something changed,
But what's so strange is that's the very night
I knew you were the one.
Remember, I sang that song for you,
And you shed a tear or two?
Funny how one moment can change everything,
But no matter how much time goes by,
There's always something that reminds me,
If even for a little while, we had it all.
Forgotten dreams...
There were so many now
It seems like it was more than
A lifetime ago.
You'll never know, but I haven't forgotten you,
Or our forgotten dreams...

Without a Word

~ ♡ ~

Looking back
On this time we've had together,
Can't make sense
Of what's happening today.
Started out with what seemed like forever,
Here we are
Trying to go our separate ways.
Without a word
We've been drifting apart.
Without a sign
You've moved out of my heart.
Without a word
You have said so many things.
Without a word...without a word...
Trying hard
To believe that we're not through,
I'm convinced that I'll always love you.
Wishing that
Certain things had never happened,
Still it's a fact
I said some things you never heard.
Is it too late
To pick up where we left off?
Are you too tired,
Or could you take the time to talk?
Does all that time not mean
A thing to you at all?
Don't understand why you hardly ever call.
Guess you said
Some things I never heard,
Without a word...

Old Love Letters

I found your old letters
Last night in the attic,
And I had to fight the tears.
The warmth that I felt from each one
Turned to magic,
And I went back in time through the years.
The pages had yellowed,
But the ink still remained,
And all of the love was the same.
The only thing missing
Was you, my old friend,
And the love that we shared way back then.
But it's still there,
I felt it in your old love letters.
That's when I knew
I'd better take the time to write it down.
I liked the sound of reading them out loud.
It's still there, and I swear that it will always be,
The love you had for me.
I felt it in your old love letters.
No one writes anymore,
We're all just so busy,
And it's such a shame to me,
Because tonight I relived
A whole year of my past.
Thanks to you it will always last.
Your words on the page painted pictures to me,
Wonder why that I didn't see,
If only I'd opened my eyes way back then
Instead of old love letters,
You might be here with me.

Grandparents

To let go of that part of you
That gave you your first breath is hard to do.
You know that there's a better place for them to be,
Still, it's so hard to see.
They gave you love,
Taught you all of what's right and wrong,
And when you cried, she sang your favorite song.
Her sweetness still lives on
In every daughter, every son.
All the families started here with just this one.
Cherish the times you share with one another,
It slips away before we know what's happened.
Remember when and where
The memories started, and keep them there
Inside your hearts with love,
Cherish this time...
There were apple pies, 4th of Julys,
Christmas days, and 'Silent Nights',
Homemade rolls, and Daddy Leonard's old cigars.
Remember all the roses in Mae-Mae's garden,
Stories of Texas, and grocery shopping,
The many times Daddy Leonard retired,
And Mae-Mae's tatting we all admired.
Sunday afternoons were part of growing up,
While they grew old and gray.
And then today, it's sad to say
How fast the time just slips away.
Cherish this time...

for Mae-Mae and Daddy Leonard

The Month of May

Today I sense the silence
As the wind blows through the trees.
I whisper sacred prayers
As they bring me to my knees.
I shed these tears of sadness,
And cry helplessly.
Time doesn't take away or heal
This missing part of me.
My mind wanders back
To the days before this tragedy.
I remember all the many things
That make me miss you now.
The love you gave to all of us
Lives on inside us still.
Sometimes I swear
You're here with me,
It's something I can feel.
I see your face inside my mind,
And hear your voice today.
I want to hold onto this moment
So it won't go away.
I remember so clearly,
Nothing has faded away.
Sometimes I reach back,
And discover something
You might say.
There is this void for all of us
That will not go away,
Still, life goes on and so will we,
I know that's what you'd say.
No sad regrets, no sad goodbyes,
No wondering 'if ' or 'why'.

I'm thankful for the time we had
Between us, you and I.
Every time the month of May
Rolls around down here,
I get so sad and cry these tears,
Because you're not here, you see.
I believe you hear the birds,
And whistle back to them.
You watch the crops,
And see the land
As it bears fruit and food.
I believe you walk today with Jesus,
And sing songs.
You watch each and every one of us
As we go on.
I know you are healthy, and happy,
And so strong.
I choose to think of good things
As this day still lingers on.
Today I picture you
Standing on that grassy hill,
Sending us kisses
From heaven
By a lonely whippoorwill.

for Daddy
9/6/'31 - 5/15/'98

Spring Hill

As I sit here in this
Ancient church,
Old ceiling fans
And wooden benches,
Generations all around,
The ivory keys
Almost worn out.
We're asked to close
Our eyes and pray,
Remember those
Who've died today.
The hymns mean
Something else to me,
I only hear your voice
And weep.
For only just a year ago,
You were here,
We didn't know
You'd leave so soon,
And there'd be room
For someone else
On this old pew.
I have no joy at all,
I feel as if
I just might fall
If I stand up
Just one more time,
Or have to fake
A smile again.
Just when I think
There are no more tears,
I can't control them,
And then I fear

Tomorrow I will still be here,
But you won't be,
Now or next year.
The wind comes through
This ancient church,
The preacher stands,
I don't hear much.
I see a wasp,
A baby cries,
The people start
To close their eyes.
My uncles, aunts,
And cousins, too,
Surround my mother,
Thinking of you.
The words don't come,
I just feel numb,
But I do remember
Where I came from,
Remember what made
Our house a home,
The love we shared,
And we do still.
I'm missing you here
At Spring Hill.

for Dad

Memorial Day

~ ♡ ~

We went back there again today
To remember those who have passed away,
As if we need a special day
To recall what words can never say.
The preacher's words don't comfort me,
Daddy's face is all I see.
My mind goes back to yesterday,
Our happy home, the things he'd say.
I remember we came here every year.
He'd lead the hymns, we'd shed a tear,
For those who'd died that very year,
But it's much worse now
Because he's not here.
I never understood that pain inside
Until my own father died.
The loss, the constant separation,
There is no kind of preparation.
Today we sang the songs,
We prayed the prayers,
But the reality is,
He's just not here.
The 'Beulah Land', the 'Sweet By and By',
The 'Meet Me on the Other Side',
Please change the hymns,
They're much too sad
For someone who just lost their Dad,
Or the wife who's had to say goodbye
To her soul mate not so long ago...
The son, or brother, sister, friend,
Or grandchild who's at the very end.
Those of us who mourn this loss,
We're not in the mood for jokes or talk.

This is holy ground we tread today,
We've come to pay tribute to those we love.
It's a sobering, sad, and lonely day.
My mom and dad sang here every year,
Now I stand next to her,
And he's not here.
There's a tear in her voice on every song
For the man who once stood here
So good and strong,
Has gone to Heaven,
And she's all alone.
I hear his voice on every hymn,
I see his face
Laughing with his friends.
I see his love for Mom, still,
I feel his strength, and know we will
See him again
Someday, somehow.
I'll come back here, same time, next year,
To honor my father's memory here.
But I don't need a special day
To remind me of the love he gave
To my mom, my brothers, and to me.
Every day's a memory
That comes back to touch my heart,
Of all those special times we had
Of which Daddy was a part.
This day is always sad for me,
And it will always be.
My daddy's buried here you see,
That's Memorial Day for me.

For George

~ ♡ ~

You gave him to us, Lord,
To raise
One cold November day.
Our blue-eyed baby boy,
So full of promise,
Full of grace.
We trusted You
Completely, God,
To guide us on our way.
To teach him of Your love,
To teach him of our faith.
We have no regrets today,
We carried out Your plan.
It seems like only yesterday,
Our little boy became a man.
His quiet strength,
His gentle touch,
His smile lights up a room,
His eyes shine through,
Straight to our soul
He is a gift, we know.
We watched him take
His first few steps,
Then watched him drive away.
Life happened much too fast,
And here we are today.
And as we sit here silently
With memories flooding in,
This day came
Much too quickly, Lord,
And Time was not our friend.

This place is sacred to us, God,
Now to our children's children.
We have no choice,
But to trust You now,
And give him back
To You.
We're not like those
Who have no hope,
For we will meet again.
And as we leave this place today,
We know that until then
We'll trust You now,
Completely, God,
To guide us on our way.
Now teach us
Of Your love,
And teach us
Of his faith.

for Aunt Ann & Uncle Gary

I'll Remember Mamaw

So many things
Come to my mind,
I think of her,
Treasures I'd find
All around her house and attic.
She kept most everything.
I'd spend the night,
We'd eat popcorn,
We'd laugh and talk,
And cry and mourn
For Papaw and for my Aunt Helen.
She grieved their deaths forever.
Losses that she suffered
Were more than some could take.
I often wondered how that
She could make it through the day.
She'd jump in her big car,
Never look back,
And drive away.
She didn't care if things were done
Around the house each day.
"Those dirty dishes
Will still be here tomorrow,"
She'd laugh and say.
I remember we would have
These great big family dinners.
There were cornbread sticks,
Fried chicken, peas and corn,
And chocolate pie.
Everyone was loud and fun,
And talking all at once.

Mamaw was quite a beauty,
And she loved to look her best.
She had a certain flare,
I guess a certain kind of zest!
I loved to play 'dress-up'
In that mink coat Papaw gave her,
With all her jewelry,
All her pearls,
Pretend that I was her.
I'll remember Mamaw
For the 'spice' she had for life,
Not for what she suffered,
Or for her pain and strife.
She was a survivor,
And she lived it gracefully,
And I'll always love her
For that part she left to me.

for Mamaw

Take My Heart

~ ♡ ~

There was nothing I could say
To change your mind that day,
Still I just kept holding on,
Knowing that we both were wrong.
The hardest part of all
Is trying to let go,
Trying to imagine you
As someone that I used to know.
Please take my heart,
Because I won't need it anymore.
Besides it's yours,
I gave it to you years before.
I loved you long before I knew your name,
And I will never be the same.
Please take my heart,
And walk away from me.
If I could take away
What's standing in between
The love we had,
And the love we'll never know again,
You know I would.
But only you can change
The things that hold you back
From being free.
If you love me,
Please just
Let me go.

This One Regret

Powerless to address the pain that grows inside,
It's too old to cut it out, and it will never die.
This life inside has taken on its own identity,
No surgeon nor modern medicine
Can break it down for me.
It started as a bad cell
From a past mistake I made.
I thought maybe it didn't take,
But it surfaced anyway.
One lie led to others, and I rediscovered 'me'
Yet, tragically, I understood
This one regret's not free.
If I'd never met you 'friend'
What might I have become?
You've pulled me down a thousand times,
And then a thousand more.
Every time a new door opened,
You were there to trip me.
Still I never recognized before
That you were more than I could carry.
All those many worthless, dreary years
Those many, many, years...
You disguised yourself as 'Mr. Right',
Careers that never would take flight,
Beautiful limitations of reality.
I listened to your choices for me,
Never had a voice myself,
And now when it's too late,
I realize you chose my fate instead of me.
All I have of yesterday
Is this one regret.

Anniversary

This night's no different from the rest
Still memories linger,
I just can't forget.
Another number on the calendar,
Another year gone by,
Still each time that I remember
A tear comes to my eye...
Not because I love you,
Not because there's no more
You and me,
Not because I'm sorry,
Not because I'm finally free,
Not because I miss you,
Not because I want you here with me.
Just because,
It's our anniversary.
That day was really special
With friends and family,
A fairytale reception
And a simple ceremony.
The vows we made meant no more
Than words said in some play,
But what a celebration,
It was our wedding day.
And each year I reflect upon
That day, and all the years beyond,
I try to find
Just one thing that was real...
And wonder how you feel
On our anniversary.

Once A Beauty Queen

She searched for years to find a man
To make her dreams come true.
Through many tears and doubt and shame,
He never came around.
She was once a beauty queen
With a million dollar smile,
But now the years of pain are showing
Right around her eyes.
She was once a beauty queen,
Now a forgotten dream.
She waited all those years,
Thinking she'd wear
A crown again.
Instead of rhinestones,
There might be
A baby, a real family.
She was once a beauty queen,
Now a forgotten dream.
They all said
She'd be the one
Who'd make it big someday.
She had everything it seemed,
Nothing was standing
In her way.
She met her match,
That perfect man,
Or so it seemed back then,
But he was angry at the world,
And she was no more than a girl.
But she was
Once a beauty queen.

Already Said Our Goodbyes

The day is finally here,
The one I've dreaded most.
The one day of the year
When I will surely shed a tear.
When I remember
The moment's finally passed,
And now at last we'll take a chance,
And go our separate ways.
Surely I've seen better days.
We've already said our goodbyes,
But it doesn't make it easier to go.
We've already said our goodbyes,
But it hurts a whole lot more
Now that I know
You're not coming back someday to me,
And I have to watch you leave,
Even though we've already
Said our goodbyes.
Never dreamed that it would hurt this much,
Never really thought we'd be out of touch.
Guess we have no choice
But to let go.
I know I told you everything I felt,
And I'll never have to
Look back and regret.
Please don't forget
I always knew how much
I meant to you,
Even though we've already
Said our goodbyes.

Yesterdays

Trying to see what's best for you,
And what is best for me.
Looking at these dreams I have,
And not reality.
Every time I see your face,
The years between us
Are erased.
It's as if we saw each other
Yesterday.
Those yesterdays
Have no place
In where we are today.
You and I chose other lives,
And went our separate ways.
Our yesterdays
Were beautiful,
And we had so much love to give.
But we can't live
Our lives
For yesterdays.
Your memories take me
Only to the places
That I choose.
I hope I never have to go
Where you and I
Both lose.
If we both could see into the future
For our fate,
Would we choose today,
Or all our
Yesterdays?

Throw Away Memories

Going through old photographs,
Love letters from my past,
Sorting out some things to keep,
And throwing out the rest.
Letting go of memories
Is painful for us all,
But there comes a time
We must let go,
We just can't keep it all.
How do you throw away memories?
Erase them from your mind?
Figure out how much to keep,
And leave the rest behind?
How do you take away that pain,
And all that wasted time?
How do you throw away memories?
Just haven't got the time...
Here's a letter I'd forgotten,
Still it makes me smile.
Wonder where you are now,
And just how many miles
Must have come between us,
Still time keeps moving on.
I hold a moment
In my hand,
It's like you've never gone.
How do you throw away memories?

Between Times

So much has happened,
And I can't erase the years.
You'd think by now
That I'd overcome my fears.
Still every time I try
To go there in my mind,
I find you there,
And wonder where you are.
Between what used to be,
And never could have been.
Between the time I gained a love,
And lost my best friend.
I can't remember when
I didn't love you
One way or another,
Between the time
That I was yours
And you were mine,
Between times...
Time has passed so quickly
That it doesn't seem that long,
I can't quite remember
What you did
That was so wrong.
It's funny how we soon forget,
Try so hard
To not regret,
Guess that we were
Never meant to be.
Between what used to be,
And never could have been.

Before You're Gone

~ ♡ ~

People come in and out
Of my life so fast,
Makes me wonder
If love can really last.
We laugh a while,
And sing some songs,
Before I know it,
They're up and gone.
Our time's so short,
Not much to spare.
Are we getting anywhere?
I want to know you
Before you're gone.
Can we just sing this one more song
Before you're gone?
Overly anxious for tomorrow,
Thinking we've got time to borrow,
But all we have is here and now.
Hope you will remember somehow,
Life is full of ups and downs,
You fall in love, and turn around,
They're gone.
We can't hold on too tightly,
You know,
There's a chance
We might let go,
And never really know
What might have been.
So just remember when
We laughed
And sang some songs.

82

Losing Faith

You took away the best of me,
So why am I to blame?
You stripped away my innocence
The day I took your name.
And as the years have slipped right by,
I still cannot recall
If I ever loved you,
Or knew you at all.
When it comes to losing faith,
I can teach the multitudes.
Gather 'round,
I'll bring you down
To reality.
Well, I can't see the future,
But I know about the past.
Listen to me loud and clear,
Love just may not last.
Sometimes late at night
I wake up scared, and all alone.
A part of you
Lives in my dreams,
I never feel at home.
If I could just erase the past
And throw away the key,
Maybe it would unlock
All this sordid mystery.
When it comes to losing faith,
I can teach the multitudes.
Gather 'round,
I'll bring you down
To reality.

A Wounded Bird

My heart lies open
Like a wounded bird
Whose desperate cry is so soft
It can barely be heard.
There's very little time
To save what's left of it,
And very little hope,
But just a little bit.
In your angel eyes
I've seen that ray of hope,
A reason to dream.
That wounded bird
I used to be
Is stronger now.
You rescued me,
And I will fly
Once more and sing,
For your eyes
Will stay with me,
And in my heart
You will remain my friend
For all eternity.
From my broken heart
To yours,
Whose pieces
Remain broken,
I cast this
One last loving thought,
And all those left unspoken.
My heart lies open
Like a wounded bird.

Just Like Old Times

~ ♡ ⌒

We laughed today,
Just like old times.
I felt your smile inside my mind.
For the first time I didn't care,
You were there and I was here.
Remembered how things used to be,
When things were good with you and me.
Remembered how you changed my life
When I knew you loved me.
It was just like old times...
We laughed 'til we cried.
It was just like old times,
I made you happy inside.
It was just like old times,
Who'd have thought
That you and I
Finally had the courage
To say goodbye...
Ever since I can remember
I've wanted it to be this way,
To leave and still be friends
Laughing at the end.
I should have known
You wouldn't let me down,
Because you never did before.
Guess that's why
I love you now
Even more.
It was just like old times...
We laughed
'Til we cried.

85

Longing

Before Winter Comes

Stay here with me.
I want to see your precious face
And hear your voice.
Spend time with me.
I'll memorize our conversations,
Laugh, and talk about vacations.
Come, stay with me
Before winter comes...
We'll go back home.
Remember special days,
The sunshine's rays,
Walks in the park,
Warm hugs in the dark,
And bear our souls to one another
Before it gets too cold outside.
Before winter comes...
Stay here with me.
I long to touch your face,
Embrace you with my heart, my eyes, my soul.
Please let me hold you now.
Give you back some love somehow,
The way you've given me.
I'd like to have you
Here with me
Before winter comes,
And we're both gone.
Before winter comes,
And there are no more songs.
Before winter comes,
And takes this
Love away...

The Wind

It's hard to tell
Which way it goes,
Sometimes it's hard
To even know.
Touches sometimes
When it's cold,
And dark and gray.
Then there are days
When it's so still,
You think it won't be long
Until it's going to rain.
And yet, it never came.
Then it blows
So we can't tell
Which direction
That it fell,
You only feel it
In a spell of mystic tones.
Then it might softly
Kiss your hair,
Try to see it,
Wonder where
And how it comes.
Windy, autumn leaves
Can only tell.
Caught up in whirlwinds
All around,
Wonder where
And how it comes.
So much like love,
Can't be held
Onto for long.

Right Here

A bit of sadness,
A taste of tears,
A love I've looked for
For many years.
To think I've found you,
Release your fears,
For I'll be with you,
Yes, I'm right here.
Can we stop time?
Will it stand still?
While you've been searching
I've been right here.
No, you're not ready, I know, my dear.
I've been your friend now,
It seems like years.
You'll go on searching
For quite some time,
And I'll be waiting
Not far behind.
I know I've found you,
I'm sure this time.
So I'll be waiting
Not far behind.
Remember laughter,
Remember tears,
And keep me with you
For many years.
And when I'm gone, Love,
I'll still be here,
You'll hear my laughter
Inside your ears.

Weary Traveler

We are travelers
On this journey
And we share
A common ground.
If we listen
For our Savior,
We can hear
The sweetest sound.
O Weary Traveler,
Come to Jesus,
He can heal
Your broken soul.
O heavy laden
And downhearted,
He will give you rest
And more.
Can you hear Him?
He is calling,
"Please come home,
My precious child."
Weary Traveler,
Let Him lead you
Down that lonely,
Extra mile.

On the Other Side

The time is drawing near,
And I must say goodbye now,
But I don't quite know how
To let you go.
You have closed your eyes,
We've said our last goodbyes,
And in this life we'll never
Have another chance
To share a laugh,
To dance a dance.
But on the other side
We'll never cry again,
Never feel the pain
That you and I felt then.
And on the other side
We'll meet again, my love,
And we will never die, or sacrifice
One more moment, on the other side.
The only way
That I can stay here now,
Is knowing that we'll
Meet again somehow.
It seems so long ago,
And some days seem so cold...
Without you here beside me,
I'm afraid to face today.
Can't you stay?
On the other side
We'll never cry again.

for Mom

Eternity

Try not to think of earthly things,
But of Eternity.
Our days are numbered
Here on earth,
And this is hard to see.
To think of him not being here
Is just too much to bear.
Just try to think you'll meet again,
Beyond all this somewhere.
There's a place
Where pain does not exist,
And suffering has no home.
A place where sickness is no more,
Where we have never gone.
A place where peace is present,
And no tears are ever shed.
A place of rest and comfort,
Where no one is ever sad.
I pray that God
Will give you strength
To face each day ahead.
This is the hardest part, I know,
Not knowing what's to come.
Try not to think
Of earthly things,
But of what you've taught me.
The home we have
On earth right now,
Will live
Eternally.

When November Comes

When November comes,
The leaves will fall again.
It won't be long, my friend,
Until this year will end.
But when November comes,
So much could change this year.
I wonder will you
Be here with me?
Remember what we've had,
Remember what we've said,
I hope you understand
Why I must go, my friend.
This choice is yours to make,
So here's your time to take.
When November comes,
I wonder will you
Be here with me?
Just a few months ago,
I didn't even know your name.
Just a little time between
Has seemed to change most everything.
I've never known this love before,
And never will again.
It's up to you what you will do,
I don't want this to end.
When November comes,
I wonder will you
Be here with me?

Wherever You Are On Christmas Eve

Alone again on Christmas Eve,
Thinking of old memories,
Remembering how things used to be
When you were here with me.
Gazing at the Christmas tree,
Wishing you were here with me.
Wonder if you're wishing you
Were here on Christmas Eve.
Wherever you are on Christmas Eve,
I'm wishing you were home with me,
Dreaming of dancing sugarplums,
Waiting on Santa Claus to come.
I'm wishing you were home with me,
Sipping on hot cocoa and humming,
You know, "Santa Claus is coming ..."
I'm missing you this Christmas Eve,
And wishing you were home with me.
Dreaming of Christmases gone by,
Feeling the tears come to my eyes,
Knowing you won't be here tonight
But in the morning,
You just might...
Waking up early just to see
What's under the mistletoe for me,
And if my Christmas wish
Came true,
To spend every
Christmas Eve
With you.

Interlude

So soft and elegant,
A sweetness all its own,
Simplistic, and yet complicated,
An in-between-time song.
Something remembered,
Perhaps forgotten,
Not too long before or after
What went right, or what went wrong.
A special moment,
Just a glance,
A mystery unsolved...
A song of love,
A hint of romance,
Perhaps a brush with fate...
An open gate, a door now closed,
A thought
For nothing more
Than now.
A circumstance
That changed somehow.
A lighter step, a magic wish,
A moonlit walk, a time to talk,
Or perhaps, to listen
For a while...
A single moment still remains,
A memory lost,
A memory gained,
A song of love
Will now remain,
Between events
So much the same.

On New Year's Eve
~ ♡ ~

The holidays have
Come and gone,
The misting rain
Is falling strong.
I'm trying now to make my plans
For the new year that's ahead.
My train of thought is failing me,
I picture your face instead.
Might as well turn off
All the lights, and go to bed.
On New Year's Eve
I still believe,
Even though you're not
Here with me,
That someday
We will be together.
And when I ring out
This old year,
Even though you won't be here,
I'll make a wish
We'll be together next year.
The decorations haven't changed,
The Christmas lights,
They're all the same,
But that Christmas cheer
Has left us now until next year.
And New Year's Day's not far away,
That midnight hour
Gets closer, too,
And my thoughts
Just seem
To all go back to you.

First Love

I heard you
Call my name today,
And when I turned around
And waved,
All those thoughts
Of yesterday
Came rushing in
Again...
I remembered our first kiss,
Remembered how
I never missed
A chance to see you,
You were my whole world.
You didn't have that much to say,
I wanted to communicate,
But looking back,
I see so clearly now...
You taught me how to speak
Without a word.
The ocean waves, the summer days,
And your sweet ways,
If we could both go back,
Would you be there?
Dreams of our first night together,
We'd live happily ever after,
Then college came,
And something changed.
I cried for days and days
It seemed.

Remember? I was home on break
And you came by,
Big mistake.
That last kiss was so tender,
I remember tasting tears,
And wondering even then
If it would ever end,
Those feelings
That I had for you,
My first love.
How did we get so caught up
In making money,
And all that stuff?
Education, moving up,
Society and 'hanging tough'.
It takes so much to just survive,
We hurry through entire lives,
And don't take time
To just sit back and think.
But when I heard you
Call my name today,
And when I turned around
And waved,
All those thoughts
Of yesterday
Came rushing in
Again...

This Old Piano

I've tried so hard to reach you,
But you're nowhere to be found.
If you knew how much I need you,
I'm sure that you would come around.
I only have myself tonight,
And this old empty house.
Tempted to call an old love
To remember how love sounds.
But instead I'll play this old piano,
And I will sing the blues,
'Cause it's been good to me,
Sweet love,
When I've been missing you.
Many nights when
I've been lonely,
So sad I couldn't sleep,
I would play this old piano
Until it made me weep.
I've pressed the keys,
Caressed it sweetly
Instead of you, my love.
The only love
That I will know
Is with these keys tonight.
So I'll play this old piano,
And I will sing the blues,
'Cause it's been good to me,
Sweet love,
When I've been missing you.

Self-esteem

It hurts to look inside myself,
And all the masks I wear.
I try to peel off one by one,
But the pain's too much to bear.
I've heard the phrase so many times,
'Don't look back, my friend.'
It came alive yesterday
As my past started unfolding.
Right before my eyes, it seemed,
A young girl and her dreams
Stood before me screaming
Of a life she'd never seen.
Then her beauty faded, songs vanished,
And tragically she disappeared.
What seemed like moments
Suddenly turned into twenty years.
It takes its toll on your body,
Certainly mind and soul,
To feel one half of you is living there,
And one half 's just not whole.
Someone explained to me of self-esteem
And what it means,
How I can heal the emptiness that lives inside of me.
After all, I only waited twenty-something years,
Procrastinated half of those,
And filled the rest with tears.
Until yesterday I kind of thought I had it all together,
Then suddenly that emptiness couldn't make it better.
It grew and grew, consumed me,
Made me doubt my mere existence.
Where is that self-esteem
When you need to go the distance?

The Bookstore

~ ♡ ~

Walked into the bookstore
To the self-help books,
Felt like all these strangers
Were giving me these looks.
Crying over certain lines,
I've felt this pain one other time,
But twice is just a little much to bear.
It's Saturday, and I'm okay,
Guess I'm reminiscing.
I knew there would come a day
When I'd be missing you.
The author says I must detach
Myself from you, and we're mismatched,
But it's a little late for that, I think.
It just so happens you're a part
Of everything that's in my heart,
And I would have to die to let you go.
So why are you the one who has to go?
And why am I the only one
Who knows just how I feel?
And where's that book to tell me how to heal?
There are books for pain and alcohol,
Co-dependents, drugs and all,
Still I can't seem to find one book for me.
The shelves are full
Of science-fiction, depression,
Drama, and addiction,
But there's not one to heal
My broken heart.
Guess I'll never know...

Patiently

♡

Patiently I wait for You
To help me through this time.
Patiently You give to me
The fullness of Your mind.
Patiently I ask You, Lord,
For peace, that I might find
The way to live like You, Lord,
So loving and so kind.
Patiently I wait for You
To find Your will for me.
You give to me so lovingly,
A purpose and a plan.
I thank You for giving me
So much of You to share.
I trust You, Lord,
To humble me,
And keep me in Your care.
Patiently I ask You, Lord,
To give me a new start.
Encourage me,
I beg You, Lord,
Today with all my heart.
I want to tell the world
Of all the love
You have for them.
For patiently
You love me, Lord,
Though I don't understand.

for Leanna

No Sad Farewells

Beyond this life
We live today,
There is a plan,
Don't be afraid.
We pass into
The arms of God,
Beyond this road
That we have trod.
No sad farewells,
No tears are shed,
No dying there,
No fear or dread,
No longing for
The ones we love,
Our gift from God
Is Heaven above.
No streets of gold,
Or mansions there,
Matter to me,
I just don't care.
I long to see
The dear face of
The one I lost,
The one I love.
No sad farewells,
No tears are shed,
No dying there,
No fear or dread,
No longing for
The ones we love,
Our gift from God
Is Heaven above.

The Pathway to Your Heart

It's been a long time
Since that road's
Been traveled.
It's dusty, and makes it
Hard to see.
If you travel in the light,
You can almost see the way,
But at night you might as well
Close your eyes,
For you may never get around
What's standing in your way.
The pathway to your heart
Is what
I'm searching for,
That secret place
Inside your soul.
Why is it so hard
To find the way?
I want to go there,
To that place.
I promise I won't stay
Too long,
But until that day,
I'll go on searching for
The pathway to your heart.

Take Some Time

Do you ever listen now
To sounds almost forgotten?
Do you ever see the sky
Turn a different
Shade of blue?
Do you ever catch a scent
Of some fragrant flower?
When's the last time that you
Felt the rain
Upon your face?
I hope you take some time today
To gaze into the wildflowers,
To listen to the birds sing,
Maybe start remembering
Days when life seemed sweeter,
Maybe just a little slower, too.
I hope you take some time today,
And I'll take some, too.
Have you seen the sunset lately,
Noticed it's purple hue?
When's the last time
That the wind
Wrapped its arms around you?
How long since the sunlight
Reached right down
And kissed your face?
How long has it been
Since you've known
This kind of place?
Take some time,
And I will, too.

106

Now and Then

Now and then
I think I hear your voice,
But you're not there.
Now and then
I hear your name
From one of our old friends.
I'll turn around, and swear
That I have seen you from a distance.
But of course this only happens
Now and then...
Now and then
I start remembering how it felt
When you loved me.
Now and then
I catch a glimpse
Of what we might have been.
And now and then
I have regrets of when I let you go,
And hope you think of me, now and then...
Now and then
I'll look through our
Old photographs
From way back when.
Now and then
I'll hear a song we slow danced to
And think of you.
There are times
I cry myself to sleep,
And think you used to be here, too.
But of course this only happens
Now and then...

To Be Content

To be content with who we are,
To feel at home inside our hearts,
To be so close
Whether we're near or far away.
To take a day, and only say
The things that matter most to us,
To take a moment of the best days that we had.
To listen closely to the sounds
Of daily things that come around,
To take the time, and realize that this is life.
To look back some, but not too often,
To feel a closeness that somehow softens
Something cold we thought
We'd let go of way back then.
To be so brave, whatever loss may come to us,
To count the cost,
To suffer through the pain
That only we alone can bear.
To understand that life is fleeting,
To waste a moment is just repeating
Old mistakes and fragile times we should let go.
One thing I know,
One thing I've learned,
It's not tomorrow, or what we'll earn,
Just be content with who we are,
To feel at home inside our hearts,
To be so close,
Whether we're near or far away.

for my family

Those Pieces

Is there something
I can say to you,
Or have I said it all?
Is there something
That I should have done,
Does it matter now at all?
Is there something now
That we could do
That never has been done?
Is there anything
You want from me,
Or would you rather be alone?
Did you understand I gave to you
Those pieces of my heart
That I had held onto so long,
I almost couldn't part
With all the love I'd held inside,
But now you hold the key.
By giving up this part of me,
I have been set free.
Those pieces of my heart
Are now a part of you,
And what you choose to do
Is only up to you.
Please take them
One by one,
No matter where you are.
Those pieces of my heart,
They now belong
To you.